I0504306

Financial Planning for Small Business Startup

The Ultimate Guide to Achieve a Successful Business

Marie R. Douglas

Copyright © 2023, Marie R. Douglas.

All rights reserved. No part of this non-fiction book may be reproduced, distributed, or transmitted in any form or by any means, including photocopying, recording, or other electronic or mechanical methods, without the prior written permission of the author, except in the case of brief quotations embodied in critical reviews and certain other noncommercial uses permitted by copyright law.

Table of Content

Introduction   4

Chapter One   7

Financial Planning Overview   7

Chapter Two   25

Estimating Startup Costs   25

Chapter Three   41

Developing a Startup Budget   41

Chapter Four   57

Securing Funding for the Startup   57

Chapter Five   71

Financial Recordkeeping and Bookkeeping   71

Conclusion   91

Introduction

Financial planning is a critical aspect of starting and running a small business. Effective financial planning helps entrepreneurs understand their current financial situation, set achievable goals, and make informed decisions to maximize profitability and long-term success. This introduction will provide an overview of financial planning for small business startups, highlighting its importance and key considerations.

Launching a small business requires careful financial planning to ensure stability and growth. Entrepreneurs must have a clear understanding of their financial resources and obligations to make informed decisions regarding investment, expenses, and revenue generation. Without proper planning, startups may face challenges such as cash flow shortages, unexpected expenses, or missed growth opportunities.

One fundamental aspect of financial planning is creating a comprehensive budget. A budget outlines projected revenues and expenses, allowing entrepreneurs to estimate their financial needs accurately. By tracking and analyzing these figures regularly, business owners can identify areas of overspending, potential cost savings, or opportunities to allocate resources more effectively.

Another crucial aspect of financial planning for startups is forecasting. Accurate financial forecasts help entrepreneurs anticipate potential financial outcomes and make informed decisions accordingly. Forecasting involves predicting future revenue streams, costs, and profitability based on market research, historical data, and industry trends. This information allows entrepreneurs to adjust their business strategies, pricing, or resource allocation to achieve their desired financial objectives.

To ensure financial stability and minimize risk, startups must establish an emergency fund. This fund serves as a buffer against unforeseen circumstances, such as equipment failure, market downturns, or unexpected expenses. By setting aside a portion of their revenue, entrepreneurs can create a safety net that protects their business from financial setbacks and provides peace of mind.Proper financial planning also involves managing business debts effectively. Startups often rely on loans or credit to fund their operations, and understanding the terms, interest rates, and repayment schedules is crucial. Entrepreneurs should develop a strategy to repay debts promptly, minimizing interest costs and improving their creditworthiness for future financial endeavors.

In addition to budgeting, forecasting, emergency funds, and debt management, small business owners should also consider the importance of cash flow management. Cash flow represents the movement of money into and out of a business, and managing it effectively is vital for day-to-day operations. Entrepreneurs must monitor their cash flow regularly, ensuring that incoming revenue is sufficient to cover expenses and that surplus funds are utilized wisely, such as reinvesting in the business or saving for future growth. A solid financial plan provides entrepreneurs with a clear roadmap for managing their resources, making informed decisions, and mitigating financial risks.

Chapter One

Financial Planning Overview

At its core, financial planning is about making informed decisions regarding money matters. It starts with a thorough assessment of the current financial situation. This involves evaluating income sources, such as salaries, investments, and any other sources of revenue, as well as analyzing expenses, including both fixed and variable costs. By understanding one's cash inflows and outflows, it becomes possible to identify areas where adjustments can be made to improve financial health.

Once the current financial situation has been evaluated, the next step in the financial planning process is to establish clear and realistic financial goals. These goals can be short-term, such as saving for a vacation, medium-term, like buying a home, or long-term, such as retirement planning. Financial goals should be specific, measurable, achievable, relevant, and time-bound (SMART). By setting specific goals, individuals can focus their efforts and make meaningful progress towards their desired outcomes.

After defining financial goals, the next phase of financial planning involves devising a strategy to achieve those goals. This typically includes creating a budget, which serves as a financial roadmap outlining income allocation and expenditure patterns. A well-designed budget considers all necessary expenses, such as housing, utilities, transportation, food, and healthcare, while also leaving room for saving and investing. The budget helps individuals prioritize spending and allocate resources effectively, ensuring that they are on track to achieve their financial objectives.

Investment planning is another crucial aspect of financial planning. It involves determining the most appropriate investment vehicles based on an individual's risk tolerance, investment horizon, and financial goals. Investments in stocks, bonds, mutual funds, real estate, or other assets may be considered. Diversification is a key principle in investment planning, as it helps spread risk and maximize potential returns. Regular monitoring and rebalancing of the investment portfolio are essential to ensure it remains aligned with one's financial goals and risk tolerance.

A crucial component of financial planning is risk management. This involves evaluating and mitigating potential risks that may impact financial stability. Insurance plays a critical role in risk management by providing protection against unforeseen events, such as accidents, illnesses, natural disasters, or death. Adequate coverage in areas like health, life, disability, and property insurance safeguards individuals and families from financial hardships in the face of unexpected circumstances.

Tax planning is yet another element of financial planning that aims to optimize tax efficiency while ensuring compliance with applicable laws and regulations. By understanding tax laws and utilizing available deductions, credits, and exemptions, individuals can minimize their tax liability and maximize their after-tax income. Effective tax planning can lead to significant savings over time, contributing to overall financial well-being.

Estate planning is an often overlooked but crucial aspect of financial planning, especially for individuals with significant assets. It involves the arrangement of one's affairs to ensure the smooth transfer of wealth and assets to intended beneficiaries while minimizing taxes and probate costs. Estate planning typically involves the creation of wills, trusts, powers of attorney, and healthcare directives, among other legal documents. By engaging in estate planning, individuals can have peace of mind knowing that their assets will be distributed according to their wishes, and their loved ones will be taken care of.

Financial planning is not a one-time event it is an ongoing process that requires regular monitoring and adjustments.

Creating a Financial Vision

Having a clear financial vision is essential for achieving long-term financial success and realizing your goals and aspirations. A financial vision provides direction, purpose, and motivation to make wise financial decisions and take the necessary actions to secure your financial future. In this article, we will explore the steps involved in creating a financial vision and how it can benefit your overall financial well-being.

1. Reflect on Your Values and Goals: Start by reflecting on your values and what you hope to achieve in life. Consider both short-term and long-term goals, such as buying a house, starting a business, saving for retirement, or funding your children's education. Understanding your values and aspirations will help shape your financial vision and align your financial decisions with what truly matters to you.

2. Assess Your Current Financial Situation: Before you can create a financial vision, it's important to assess your current financial situation. Make a list of your earnings, spending, possessions, and debts. Evaluate your spending habits, debt levels, and savings rate. This evaluation will provide a baseline from which you can develop your financial vision and identify areas for improvement.

3. Define Your Financial Priorities: Once you have a clear understanding of your values, goals, and current financial situation, prioritize your financial objectives. Consider which goals are most important to you and rank them accordingly. It's important to be realistic and prioritize goals that are achievable based on your resources and timeframes.

4. Set SMART Financial Goals: SMART goals are specific, measurable, achievable, relevant, and time-bound. Use this framework to set your financial goals. For example, rather than saying, "I want to save more money," a SMART goal would be, "I will save $10,000 over the next 12 months by setting aside $800 each month. Setting SMART objectives makes them more concrete and offers a clear path to success

5. Visualize Your Ideal Financial Future: Close your eyes and visualize your ideal financial future. Imagine yourself living a life of financial abundance, free from debt, and enjoying the fruits of your labor. Visualizing your financial success creates a positive mindset and reinforces your motivation to work towards your financial vision.

6. Develop an Action Plan: A financial vision without an action plan is merely a dream. Break down your financial goals into smaller,

manageable steps and develop an action plan to achieve them. For each goal, outline the specific actions you need to take, allocate resources, and set deadlines. This will help you stay focused and accountable throughout your financial journey.

7. Seek Professional Advice: If you're unsure about how to create a financial vision or develop an action plan, consider seeking advice from a financial professional. They can provide expert guidance tailored to your specific circumstances and help you make informed decisions. A financial advisor or planner can assist you in creating a comprehensive financial roadmap aligned with your vision.

8. Review and Adjust Regularly: A financial vision is not set in stone. Life circumstances change, goals evolve, and external factors influence your financial situation. It's important to review your financial vision regularly and make necessary adjustments. Schedule regular check-ins to assess your progress, reevaluate your goals, and make any required modifications to your action plan.

9. Stay Committed and Motivated: Building a strong financial future requires discipline, perseverance, and staying motivated. Keep your financial vision at the forefront of your mind and remind yourself regularly of the reasons why you're pursuing it. Celebrate milestones along the

way and seek support from friends, family, or a financial accountability partner to stay on track.

10. Embrace Financial Education: Educate yourself about personal finance and investment strategies. The more knowledgeable you are, the better equipped you'll be to make informed financial decisions that align with your vision.

Defining Business Goals and Objectives

Financial planning plays a crucial role in the success and sustainability of any business. It involves setting clear goals and objectives that provide direction and purpose for the organization's financial activities. By establishing well-defined goals and objectives, businesses can effectively allocate resources, measure performance, and make informed decisions to achieve long-term financial success. In this article, we will delve into the importance of defining business goals and objectives for financial planning and explore key considerations in the process.

Business Goals: Setting the Direction

Business goals are broad, overarching statements that articulate what an organization aims to achieve in the long run. They represent the destination towards which all financial planning efforts are directed. Goals provide clarity, focus, and a sense of purpose, serving as a compass for decision-making and resource allocation.

When defining business goals, it is crucial to ensure they are specific, measurable, attainable, relevant, and time-bound (SMART).

Examples of business goals may include increasing market share, expanding into new markets or product lines, improving profitability, enhancing customer satisfaction, or establishing a strong brand presence. These goals serve as the foundation for developing more specific and actionable financial objectives.

Business Objectives: Translating Goals into Measurable Targets

Financial objectives are derived from business goals and outline the specific targets and metrics that businesses aim to achieve within a defined timeframe. They provide a roadmap for financial planning by breaking down the broader goals into smaller, quantifiable steps. Financial objectives should be aligned with the overall business strategy and take into account the organization's strengths, weaknesses, opportunities, and threats.

Key financial objectives often encompass areas such as revenue growth, cost management, liquidity management, profitability, return on investment (ROI), cash flow, debt reduction, and working capital optimization. .Each goal must be clear, quantifiable, doable, pertinent, and time-bound. For example, a financial objective could be to increase annual revenue by 10% over the next fiscal year or reduce operating expenses by 5% within six months.

Considerations for Defining Goals and Objectives

Defining business goals and objectives for financial planning requires careful consideration and analysis. The following are some essential considerations for the procedure:

Business Environment: Assess the internal and external factors that may impact the business's financial performance. Consider market conditions, industry trends, regulatory changes, competitive landscape, and customer preferences. Understanding the business environment helps in setting realistic goals and objectives.

Financial Analysis: Conduct a comprehensive analysis of the organization's financial health, including historical financial statements, key performance indicators (KPIs), and financial ratios. Identify areas of strength and weakness to determine where improvements are needed. This analysis serves as a basis for setting meaningful and relevant financial objectives.

Resource Allocation: Consider the resources available to the organization, including capital, human resources, technology, and infrastructure. Assess the financial implications of pursuing different goals and objectives and ensure that they are feasible within the available resources.

Risk Management: Identify and evaluate potential risks and uncertainties that may impact the achievement of financial goals and objectives. Develop strategies to mitigate these risks and establish contingency plans. Financial planning should incorporate risk management practices to ensure the business's financial stability and resilience.

Monitoring and Review: Regularly monitor and review the progress towards achieving financial objectives. Establish key performance indicators (KPIs) and implement reporting mechanisms to track performance against targets. Adjust goals and objectives if necessary based on changing circumstances or emerging opportunities.

Benefits of Defining Business Goals and Objectives for Financial Planning

Defining clear and well-aligned business goals and objectives for financial planning offers several benefits

1. Clarity and Focus: Setting clear goals and objectives helps provide a sense of direction and purpose for the business. It ensures that everyone involved understands what the organization is striving to achieve financially.

2. Strategic Decision-Making: Clearly defined goals enable better decision-making processes. Financial planning can be aligned with the specific objectives, allowing businesses to allocate resources effectively and prioritize

investments based on their potential impact on achieving the goals.

3. Resource Allocation: Setting goals and objectives helps determine the resources required to attain them. Financial planning becomes more targeted and efficient as businesses allocate funds, personnel, and other resources in a manner that supports the defined goals.

4. Performance Measurement: Goals and objectives provide benchmarks for measuring the financial performance of a business. By comparing actual results with the desired outcomes, organizations can track their progress and identify areas for improvement or course correction.

5. Motivation and Accountability: Clearly articulated goals and objectives create a shared vision among employees, fostering motivation and alignment towards a common financial target. It also enhances accountability, as individuals and teams can be held responsible for their contributions to achieving the defined goals.

6. Adaptability and Flexibility: Financial planning tied to specific goals enables businesses to adapt and respond to changes in the market or internal environment. By regularly evaluating the goals and adjusting the financial plans accordingly, organizations can stay agile and responsive to emerging opportunities or challenges.

7. Investor Confidence: Defining business goals and objectives demonstrates a proactive and strategic approach to financial management. This can enhance investor confidence, as stakeholders can see that the organization has a clear roadmap for financial success, increasing the likelihood of attracting funding and support.

Overall, defining business goals and objectives for financial planning facilitates strategic decision-making, resource allocation, performance measurement, motivation, adaptability, and investor confidence, all of which contribute to the long-term financial success of the organization

Key Financial Planning Considerations

Starting a small business can be an exciting endeavor, but it requires careful financial planning to ensure its success. Financial planning plays a crucial role in helping small business owners establish a strong foundation, manage resources effectively, and navigate potential challenges. This article explores the key aspects of financial planning that entrepreneurs should consider when launching a small business startup.

Create a Comprehensive Business Plan: A solid business plan is the foundation for any successful startup. It serves as a roadmap that outlines the business's objectives, strategies, target market, and financial projections. In the financial section of the business plan, entrepreneurs should include a startup budget, projected income statements, balance sheets, and cash flow forecasts. These financial projections provide a clear picture of the business's financial health and help secure funding from investors or lenders.

Establish a Realistic Budget: Developing a comprehensive budget is essential for small business startups. It helps entrepreneurs estimate and allocate resources effectively, manage expenses, and track financial performance. When creating a budget, consider fixed costs (rent, utilities), variable costs (inventory, marketing), and one-time expenses (equipment, licenses). Regularly review and adjust the budget as the business grows and evolves.

Secure Adequate Funding: Securing adequate funding is often a major challenge for small business startups. Consider various funding options, such as personal savings, loans from banks or credit unions, crowdfunding, angel investors, or venture capital. Thoroughly research and assess the pros and cons of each option to determine the most suitable funding sources for your business. It's crucial to have a clear understanding of the costs associated with each funding method, including interest rates, repayment terms, and equity dilution.

Implement Sound Financial Record-Keeping: Accurate financial record-keeping is essential for small business startups to monitor cash flow, track expenses, and comply with tax regulations. Choose appropriate accounting software and establish standardized processes for invoicing, receipts, and expense tracking. Regularly reconcile bank statements, update financial records, and maintain organized documentation to ensure financial transparency and facilitate decision-making.

Manage Cash Flow Effectively: Managing cash flow is vital for the survival and growth of small business startups. Create cash flow forecasts to estimate incoming and outgoing cash over a specific period. Monitor accounts receivable, accounts payable, and inventory levels to ensure timely payments and avoid liquidity issues. Implement strategies to improve cash flow, such as offering early payment discounts or negotiating favorable payment terms with suppliers. Maintain a cash reserve to handle unexpected expenses or revenue fluctuations.

Monitor and Evaluate Key Performance Indicators: Identifying and monitoring key performance indicators (KPIs) is crucial for assessing the financial health and success of a small business startup. Determine relevant KPIs based on industry benchmarks and business goals. Common financial KPIs include gross profit margin, net profit margin, return on investment, and customer acquisition cost. Regularly analyze and evaluate these

KPIs to identify areas for improvement and make informed strategic decisions.

Financial planning is a critical component of small business startup success. By creating a comprehensive business plan, establishing a realistic budget, securing adequate funding, implementing sound financial record-keeping, managing cash flow effectively, and monitoring key performance indicators, entrepreneurs can lay a strong foundation for their business's financial stability and growth. Seeking professional advice from accountants or financial advisors can provide valuable insights and guidance throughout the financial planning process. With proper financial planning, small business startups can increase their chances of long-term viability and prosperity.

Chapter Two

Estimating Startup Costs

Starting a small business is an exciting endeavor that requires careful planning and financial preparation. One crucial aspect of this process is estimating startup costs accurately. Without a clear understanding of the initial investment required, it can be challenging to develop a viable financial plan for your startup. In this article, we will explore the key considerations and steps involved in estimating startup costs for financial planning in small business startups.

Defining Startup Costs: Startup costs refer to the expenses incurred before a business begins its normal operations. These costs typically include both one-time expenses and initial operating expenses. One-time expenses cover items such as market research, legal fees, equipment purchases, and initial inventory. Initial operating expenses include rent, utility deposits, marketing expenses, and salaries for the first few months.

Research and Analysis: Before estimating startup costs, thorough research and analysis are necessary. Begin by conducting market research to understand the industry and competition. This research will help you identify key expenses required to establish and operate your business successfully. Additionally, analyze similar businesses in your industry to gain insights into their startup costs and operational expenses.

Identify Key Cost Categories: To estimate startup costs effectively, it is essential to identify and categorize the different expenses involved. Common categories include:

a) Legal and Regulatory Costs: These include fees for business registration, permits, licenses, and professional services like legal advice and trademark registration.

b) Equipment and Supplies: This category covers the cost of purchasing or leasing equipment, machinery, furniture, fixtures, and initial supplies required for your business operations.

c) Technology and Software: Consider the cost of computer hardware, software licenses, website development, and other technology-related expenses.

d) Marketing and Advertising: Include expenses related to branding, website design, advertising campaigns, social media marketing, and any other promotional activities.

e) Facilities and Utilities: Estimate costs for renting or leasing office or retail space, security deposits, utilities setup fees, and ongoing utility bills.

f) Inventory: If your business involves selling physical products, calculate the initial cost of inventory required to stock your shelves.

g) Salaries and Benefits: Consider the salaries, wages, and benefits for yourself and any employees during the startup phase.

h) Professional Services: Account for fees charged by consultants, accountants, bookkeepers, and other professionals you may need to hire.

i) Insurance: Estimate the cost of insurance coverage required for your business, such as liability insurance, property insurance, and workers' compensation insurance.

j) Miscellaneous Expenses: Include any additional expenses not covered by the above categories, such as travel costs, office supplies, and initial training or certifications.

Estimate Costs for Each Category: Once you have identified the key cost categories, it's time to estimate the expenses associated with each one. Start by researching market prices and obtaining quotes from vendors and service providers. For equipment and supplies, consider whether purchasing or leasing is more cost-effective. Take into account any ongoing maintenance or subscription fees for software and technology services.

Create a Startup Budget: With cost estimates in hand, it's time to create a comprehensive startup budget. A budget serves as a roadmap for managing your finances and helps ensure that you allocate resources effectively. Use a spreadsheet or budgeting software to organize and track your estimated costs for each category. Consider adding a contingency fund of around 10-20% of the total estimated startup costs to account for unforeseen expenses.

Review and Revise: Once you have prepared your initial budget, review and revise it multiple times to ensure accuracy. Seek feedback from industry experts, mentors, or business advisors who can provide valuable insights. Take into account any additional expenses or overlooked costs during this review

Identifying Initial Investment Requirements

Starting a small business requires careful financial planning to ensure its success and long-term sustainability. One crucial aspect of this planning is determining the initial investment requirements. Understanding the financial needs of a startup is essential for securing funding, allocating resources, and setting realistic goals. In this article, we will discuss the key steps involved in identifying the initial investment requirements for a small business startup.

Conduct Thorough Market Research: Before diving into financial planning, it is essential to conduct thorough market research. This step helps in understanding the industry landscape, target market, and potential competition. By analyzing market trends, customer preferences, and industry benchmarks, you can make informed decisions regarding your initial investment needs. Identify the cost of acquiring assets, equipment, and supplies specific to your business. Additionally, consider expenses related to market entry, branding, and marketing activities.

Develop a Detailed Business Plan:A comprehensive business plan is a cornerstone of any successful startup. It serves as a roadmap for your business and helps attract investors or lenders. Within the business plan, you should outline your company's vision, mission, products or services, target market, and marketing strategies. Moreover, include a detailed financial section that outlines your startup costs, revenue projections, and anticipated expenses. A well-structured business plan will enable you to estimate the initial investment requirements accurately.

Identify Startup Costs: Startup costs refer to the one-time expenses associated with launching a new business. These costs typically include:

a. Legal and Licensing Fees: Registering your business, obtaining permits and licenses, and securing intellectual property rights may require legal assistance and involve fees.

b. Equipment and Supplies: Determine the equipment, machinery, furniture, and supplies needed to operate your business. Research and obtain quotes from suppliers to estimate the costs accurately.

c. Technology and Software: Consider the technology infrastructure required, such as computers, software licenses, website development, and online platforms.

d. Real Estate: If your business requires a physical location, calculate the costs associated with lease or purchase, renovation, utilities, and insurance.

e. Initial Inventory: For businesses selling products, determine the initial inventory required to meet demand during the initial period. Calculate the cost of sourcing or manufacturing the inventory.

f. Marketing and Advertising: Allocate funds for branding, advertising campaigns, website development, and promotional materials.

g. Professional Services: Consider costs related to hiring professionals, such as lawyers, accountants, or consultants, for advice on legal, financial, or operational matters.

h. Working Capital: Set aside funds for day-to-day operational expenses, such as rent, utilities, salaries, and marketing, until your business becomes self-sustaining.

Estimate Pre-launch and Operating Expenses: In addition to startup costs, it is crucial to estimate pre-launch and operating expenses. These ongoing costs may include:

a. Salaries and Wages: Determine the compensation for employees, including yourself, if applicable. Consider employee benefits and payroll taxes.

b. Rent and Utilities: Calculate the monthly rent or mortgage payment for your business location, along with utility costs like electricity, water, internet, and telephone.

c. Insurance: Assess the types of insurance coverage required for your business, such as liability insurance, property insurance, or workers' compensation insurance.

d. Marketing and Advertising: Allocate a budget for ongoing marketing and advertising efforts to promote your products or services and attract customers.

e. Maintenance and Repairs: Factor in costs for maintaining and repairing equipment, machinery, and other assets essential to your business operations.

f. Administrative Expenses: Include expenses related to office supplies, professional fees, subscriptions, licenses, and other administrative costs.

g. Inventory and Raw Materials: If applicable, estimate the cost of replenishing inventory or purchasing raw materials for manufacturing product

h. Taxes: Incorporating taxes as part of the initial investment requirements is crucial for small business startups. Understanding and planning for tax obligations will help avoid surprises and ensure compliance with legal requirements.

Assessing One-Time Expenses

Assessing One-Time Expenses for Small Business Startup is a Vital Step in Financial Planning

Financial planning is a crucial aspect of launching a small business startup. While day-to-day expenses are important, one-time expenses play a significant role in determining the success and sustainability of your venture. These expenses, incurred at the outset of your business, can have a long-lasting impact on your cash flow and profitability. In this article, we will delve into the importance of assessing one-time expenses and provide insights into how you can effectively plan and manage them for the financial health of your small business startup.

The Significance of One-Time Expenses

One-time expenses encompass a wide range of costs that are typically incurred only once during the initial stages of setting up a small business. These expenses can include incorporation fees, licenses and permits, equipment and machinery purchases, office setup costs, branding and marketing expenses, website development, legal fees, and initial inventory purchases, among others. Ignoring or underestimating these expenses can lead to severe financial setbacks and potential failure.

Assessing One-Time Expenses

To ensure accurate financial planning, it is essential to thoroughly assess and account for one-time expenses. Start by conducting thorough market research and developing a comprehensive business plan. This will help you identify and estimate the various expenses you are likely to encounter. Consider seeking advice from industry experts, business mentors, or financial advisors to gain insights and expertise in your specific field.

Create a detailed budget that incorporates all anticipated one-time expenses. Categorize the expenses into different sections, such as legal and administrative, technology and equipment, marketing and advertising, and operational setup costs. Assign realistic cost estimates to each category based on your research and expert guidance.

Additionally, be prepared for unexpected expenses by setting aside a contingency fund. It is common for unforeseen costs to arise during the early stages of business operations, and having a safety net can help you navigate through these challenges without jeopardizing your financial stability.

Managing One-Time Expenses

Careful management of one-time expenses is critical to maintaining financial stability. Consider the following strategies:

Prioritize expenses: Rank your expenses based on their necessity and potential impact on your business. Allocate resources to essential items first and defer less critical expenses if necessary.

Seek cost-effective options: Research and compare prices for equipment, supplies, services, and contractors. Negotiate with vendors and suppliers to obtain the best possible deals and discounts. Consider leasing equipment or sharing resources with other businesses to reduce upfront costs.

Leverage technology: Embrace cost-effective digital solutions for tasks such as bookkeeping, marketing, and customer relationship management. Cloud-based software and automation tools can save both time and money, enabling efficient operations while minimizing expenses.

Explore alternative financing options: Traditional bank loans may not always be accessible or feasible for small business startups. Consider crowdfunding, grants, angel investors, or microloans tailored for small businesses. Thoroughly research the available options and their associated terms and conditions.

Review legal and compliance requirements: Understand the legal and regulatory obligations specific to your industry. Complying with licenses, permits, taxes, and insurance requirements can help avoid penalties and potential legal issues in the future.

Monitor and adjust your budget: Regularly review your expenses and compare them to your initial budget. Determine where you can make savings or resource reallocations. Flexibility and adaptability are key to maintaining financial stability during the early stages of your business.

Assessing one-time expenses is an essential step in financial planning for small business startups. By thoroughly researching, estimating, and managing these expenses, you can ensure a solid foundation for your venture. Prioritizing and seeking cost-effective solutions, leveraging technology, and exploring

Calculating Ongoing Operational Costs

When starting a small business, it is essential to set up a financial plan. As part of this process, it is also important to consider how to calculate and plan for ongoing operational costs. Operational costs are those expenses related to running the day-to-day operations of a business such as payroll, rent, utilities, and supplies. Having an understanding of and accounting for these costs is critical in setting up a financial plan because these costs are ongoing, and not addressing them can have significant implications for a business.

Operational costs can be broken down into two types: fixed and variable costs. Fixed costs are costs that remain consistent regardless of production; examples of such costs are rent, payroll, utilities, insurance, and taxes. Variable costs, on the other hand, often vary with the production level or the use of certain resources; examples of these costs are materials, supplies, and fuel.

To accurately forecast ongoing operational costs, a business must first analyze its current operations. This includes obtaining detailed records and an understanding of the business's processes, and identifying the recurring costs and expenses associated with them. For instance, for a manufacturing business, it is essential to understand the cost of raw material, the cost of labour and electricity used to run the machines, and the shipping and handling fees associated with the sale of the product. It is essential to look at the data in detail as small variations can add up to significant costs if unaccounted for. Additionally, when doing the analysis, it is important to factor in any potential seasonal fluctuations in costs and prices.

Once an understanding of the operational costs is gained, this information can be used to project future costs and expenses. A business can use this data to build both budgets and cost estimations. To build a budget, the reported data can be used to build an understanding of what the expenses are and what the estimated expenses for the following year will be. Additionally, the estimated costs can then be broken down into quarterly or monthly estimates based on the business's individual needs. Once a budget is established, it can be revised over the course of the year to account for any variations or unforeseen expenses.

When estimating the operational costs of a business, it is also important to consider other non-recurring or one-time costs associated with changes to operations or setting up infrastructure. For example, if a business is making an upgrade to its IT infrastructure, installing a new software system to improve operations, or making any other changes that require an initial investment, these costs need to be factored in. To ensure accuracy in the estimates, it is important to discuss these investments and costs with experts in the field to ensure that the cost projections are accurate.

With a good understanding of the expected operational costs, it is easier to build a more accurate financial plan that includes estimates of income and expenditures. Additionally, having a strong understanding of the expenses associated with running the business helps minimize the potential for unexpected costs that can affect the profitability of the business.

Calculating and accounting for operational costs is an essential part of creating a financial plan for a small business. Having a detailed understanding of the process helps build more accurate financial projections and budgets that can be used to make informed decisions for the business. Additionally, it is important to not only consider recurring costs and expenses but to also factor in any non-recurring investments that may affect the cost of operations. With accurate data and projections in place, a business is in a better position to make wise financial decisions.

Chapter Three

Developing a Startup Budget

Starting a business comes with a lot of risks, and careful financial planning is essential. A startup budget outlines all of the costs associated with starting a business and helps identify and allocate funds to finance the start-up, operating costs, and growth. It also serves as a roadmap for making informed decisions regarding the financial well-being of the business. Developing a startup budget for financial planning for small business start-up requires foresight, research, and careful consideration of both short-term and long-term expenses.

Types of expense

The most basic expenses for any business whether a start-up or an established firm include the costs associated with the actual physical location of the business. These costs may include rent, utilities, repairs, and insurance. Depending on the number of employees, payroll is also a significant expense to consider. In addition to salaries, this also includes payroll taxes, health insurance premiums, and other taxes and benefits. Among the other costs associated with the business are employee training expenses, as well as any other outsourced services, such as accounting and research. Inventory and supply costs are also essential elements to take into account when developing a startup budget. Marketing should also be a considered expense for any business, as new business typically requires some degree of marketing to reach customers. This may include advertising, promotions, public relations, and other efforts designed to boost the company's visibility. Finally, any miscellaneous expenses associated with the business should also be included in the budget.

Start-up expenses: When developing a budget for a small business start-up, potential start-up expenses should be taken into account. This may include costs such as the initial licensing and permitting fees, registration costs with federal or state agencies, purchase and installation of furniture and equipment, costs associated with the development of the company website, and other costs related to the initial set-up. Depending on the type of business, start-up fees may include legal and accounting fees. Other start-up expenses that may need to be budgeted for are the purchase of any inventory, supplies, software, and other investments necessary to get the business running. Related to start-up expenses, human capital is also an area that needs to be explored and included in the budget. This category includes wages and salaries, employee benefits, bonuses, as well as job training expenses. Any employees hired should be fully prepared to handle the job tasks and responsibilities the company requires, and any necessary training must be taken into account.

Operating expenses: After the start-up costs, the next important part of any budget is operational costs. This includes recurring expenses that the business will incur on an ongoing basis, such as rent and utilities, payroll, and advertising. Other operational expenses may include legal and accounting fees, loan interest payments, taxes, and any other expenses necessary to keep the business running. It is important to note that any changes to the business, such as new hires, additional inventory, or the acquisition of new equipment, can also affect a small business's budget. It is essential to take into account any changes to the budget when planning for a business's growth.

Growth expenses: Growth expenses are intended to provide the necessary funding to scale up a business. Growth expenses may include investments for the expansion of existing businesses or the launch of new products and services. These investments may include marketing campaigns, equipment, and personnel. Additionally, depending on the nature of the business, growth expenses may also include investments in technology upgrades, new software, and other software licenses. It is important to take into account any technological advancement that is necessary for the business to stay competitive.

Cash flow

Cash flow is an important component of any business as it shows the actual amount of money that comes into and out of the business. This helps the entrepreneur monitor the inflow and outflow of money and identify any potential cash flow issues. This also helps determine the amount of cash retained by the company and the amount of funding that is needed. Cash flow should be closely monitored to ensure that the budget remains on track and there are funds available for any unanticipated expenses.

Creating a budget is a vital part of financial planning for any small business start-up as it provides a roadmap for the business to follow. It requires foresight, research, and careful consideration of both short-term and long-term expenses. The budget should account for all of the expected start-up, operating, and growth expenses to ensure the business's financial health. Additionally, closely monitoring the cash flow is necessary to avoid any potential cash flow issues. With proper financial planning, small business start-ups can ensure they are taking all the necessary steps to ensure their success.

Creating a Budget Framework

Creating a budget framework includes forecasting cash flow, setting budgets and objectives, planning spending, and managing investment portfolios. This framework is the foundation of any successful business strategy and is essential to a business's survival, growth, and success.

Creating a Budget Framework

The first step in creating a budget framework for a small business is to forecast cash flow. This involves estimating the company's income and expenses for the upcoming fiscal year. It is important to consider any potential changes that may occur in the business during the year and to factor seasonal sales or other cyclical fluctuations into the cash flow projections. Cash flow should be balanced against the forecasted company profits to ensure that the budget is realistic and achievable.

Once the cash flow estimates are complete, the next step is to set budgets and objectives. These should include a clear picture of the short-term and long-term financial goals of the company, such as increasing revenue, reducing costs, and increasing profits. The budgets should provide detailed guidelines on how to allocate funds for day-to-day operations, capital investments, and other expenditures. The budget should also include a timeline for achieving the objectives, outlining benchmarks at each stage and contingencies in the event financial goals are not met.

After setting budgets and objectives, the next step is to plan spending. This involves allocating funds for specific projects and managing all associated expenses. This includes identifying and prioritizing major expenses such as employee salaries, rent and operating expenses, and researching more affordable alternatives. This is also a good time to review any contracts with suppliers and to consider any new or alternative vendors that may provide better value for money.

The last step is to manage investment portfolios. This involves selecting the most appropriate funds to meet the company's investment objectives. Consideration should be given to the risk appetite of the investor, the amount of funds available, the investment horizon, and the tax implications of different investments. Additionally, investment decisions should be monitored regularly to ensure that they are staying on track and to make any necessary adjustments.

Creating a budget framework is essential for any small business startup. It provides a blueprint for financial planning and helps ensure that the business is on the right track. This framework should include forecasting cash flow, setting budgets and objectives, planning spending, and managing investment portfolios. By considering these steps and implementing a well thought out budgeting plan, small business owners can ensure that their startup will have the best chance of success.

Allocating Funds to Key Business Areas

Effective allocation of funds is crucial for the success and growth of any business. It involves the process of distributing financial resources to different areas of the organization based on their strategic importance and potential for generating returns. By allocating funds wisely, businesses can optimize their operations, support innovation, and drive sustainable growth. This article explores the key considerations and best practices for allocating funds to various business areas.

Financial Planning and Budgeting: The first step in allocating funds is to develop a comprehensive financial plan and budget. This involves setting financial goals, forecasting revenues and expenses, and determining the overall financial resources available for allocation. The budgeting process helps businesses prioritize their spending and identify the key areas that require funding.

Strategic Priorities: Allocating funds should align with the organization's strategic priorities. Each business area must be evaluated based on its potential for contributing to the overall objectives and goals of the company. This requires a thorough understanding of the market, customer needs, competitive landscape, and internal capabilities. By focusing on strategic priorities, businesses can ensure that their financial resources are allocated to areas that have the highest impact on performance and growth.

Core Business Operations: Allocating funds to core business operations is essential to maintain and enhance the day-to-day functioning of the organization. This includes funding for production, inventory management, logistics, quality control, and customer service. Investments in these areas can improve operational efficiency, reduce costs, and enhance customer satisfaction. Allocating funds to core operations should be a top priority for businesses, as they form the foundation for sustainable growth.

Research and Development (R&D): Innovation is crucial for businesses to stay competitive in today's rapidly evolving markets. Allocating funds to research and development activities allows organizations to drive product and service innovation, explore new technologies, and create a pipeline of future offerings. R&D investments can lead to the development of new revenue streams, improved products, and increased market share. Businesses should allocate funds to R&D based on their industry dynamics and the importance of innovation in their strategic plans.

Marketing and Sales: Effective marketing and sales activities are vital for driving customer acquisition, retention, and revenue growth. Allocating funds to marketing initiatives such as advertising, promotion, branding, and market research can help businesses reach their target audience, create brand awareness, and generate leads. Sales force training, incentives, and infrastructure should also be adequately funded to ensure a high level of sales productivity. The allocation of funds to marketing and sales should be based on market dynamics, competitive positioning, and growth targets.

Human Resources and Talent Development: Allocating funds to human resources (HR) and talent development is crucial for building a skilled and motivated workforce. Investments in recruitment, training, performance management, and employee benefits can help attract and retain top talent, enhance employee productivity, and foster a positive work culture. HR initiatives that focus on talent development and succession planning are particularly important for the long-term sustainability of the organization. Businesses should allocate funds to HR activities based on their workforce needs and talent strategy.

Technology and Infrastructure: In today's digital age, allocating funds to technology and infrastructure is essential for businesses to stay competitive and adapt to changing market dynamics. This includes investments in hardware, software, cybersecurity, data analytics, and infrastructure upgrades. Technology investments can improve operational efficiency, enhance decision-making capabilities, and enable businesses to leverage emerging technologies such as artificial intelligence and cloud computing. Allocating funds to technology and infrastructure should be based on the organization's digital strategy and the potential for technology-driven innovation.

Expansion and Growth Initiatives: Allocating funds to expansion and growth initiatives is crucial for businesses aiming to enter new markets, launch new products, or acquire other companies. These initiatives require significant financial resources for market research, product development, marketing, distribution

Monitoring and Adjusting the Budget

Monitoring and adjusting the budget is a crucial aspect of financial management for individuals, businesses, and organizations. A budget serves as a financial roadmap, outlining income and expenses, and provides a framework for achieving financial goals. However, simply creating a budget is not enough; it requires ongoing monitoring and adjustments to ensure its effectiveness and adaptability to changing circumstances.We will explore the importance of monitoring and adjusting the budget and discuss practical strategies to achieve financial stability and success.

Monitoring the budget involves regularly tracking income and expenses to assess whether the actual financial performance aligns with the planned budget. It provides a snapshot of the financial health and allows individuals or organizations to identify potential issues or discrepancies early on. By monitoring the budget, one can quickly identify overspending, revenue shortfalls, or unexpected expenses, and take appropriate actions to address them promptly.

There are several key benefits to monitoring the budget. First and foremost, it enables financial awareness and accountability. When individuals or organizations actively monitor their budget, they gain a clear understanding of their financial situation, enabling informed decision-making. It helps identify areas of excessive spending or inefficiencies, allowing for adjustments and cost-saving measures. Moreover, monitoring the budget provides insights into trends and patterns, facilitating future financial planning and forecasting.

To effectively monitor the budget, it is essential to establish a systematic tracking process. This can be done through various methods, such as maintaining detailed financial records, utilizing budgeting software or apps, or leveraging online banking tools. The chosen approach should align with the specific needs and preferences of the individual or organization. Regularly reviewing bank statements, receipts, and invoices, and comparing them against the budgeted amounts, helps identify any discrepancies and enables swift corrective actions.

Once potential issues are identified through monitoring, it becomes crucial to adjust the budget accordingly. Adjustments involve making necessary modifications to income and expense allocations to better align with financial goals and changing circumstances. It allows for flexibility and ensures that the budget remains realistic and achievable.

When adjusting the budget, it is essential to prioritize expenses based on their importance and urgency. Fixed expenses, such as rent or mortgage payments, utility bills, and debt obligations, should be given top priority. Discretionary expenses, on the other hand, can be adjusted to accommodate changes in financial circumstances. By reevaluating and reprioritizing expenses, individuals or organizations can optimize their budget and allocate resources where they are most needed.

Adjustments to the budget may also involve identifying opportunities for cost savings. This can be achieved by exploring alternative suppliers or service providers, negotiating better terms or discounts, or eliminating non-essential expenses. Regularly reviewing and optimizing expenses can significantly contribute to financial stability and create opportunities for savings or investments.

In addition to expense adjustments, monitoring the budget may also reveal the need for income modifications. If the budget indicates a consistent shortfall in revenue, individuals or organizations may need to explore additional income streams or seek opportunities for career advancement or business growth. Alternatively, if income exceeds expectations, it can be wise to allocate the surplus towards debt repayment, savings, or investments to further enhance financial stability and future growth.

To ensure the effectiveness of budget adjustments, it is crucial to establish a feedback loop. Regularly reviewing the impact of adjustments on financial performance and comparing it to the initial budget can provide valuable insights. If adjustments prove successful, they can be incorporated into future budget planning. However, if adjustments do not yield the desired results, it may be necessary to reassess the approach and make further modifications.

Furthermore, it is essential to consider external factors that may impact the budget. Economic conditions, industry trends, regulatory changes, or personal circumstances can all influence the financial landscape. By staying informed and aware of these factors, individuals or organizations can proactively anticipate and respond to potential challenges or opportunities, making necessary adjustments to their budget and financial strategies

Chapter Four

Securing Funding for the Startup

For many entrepreneurs, launching a small business requires more than just a good idea. It also takes working capital to purchase equipment, inventory, payroll expenses, and other costs associated with running a business. It can be difficult for a small business to acquire the funding they need to get their business off the ground and running. Fortunately, there are a variety of sources from which to secure funding for a small business.

The most common source of small business funding is a bank loan. Banks offer loans to small business owners, allowing them to borrow money with the promise of paying the money back, usually with interest. Many banks have specific loan programs designed for small business owners, which can make securing a loan easier than it might be if the business owner was borrowing money for any other purpose. The downside to bank loans is that many banks require a strong credit history in order to qualify for a loan, so business owners with poor credit may find it difficult to get a bank loan.

Another source of small business funding is angel investors. Angel investors are individuals with funds to lend (usually wealthy individuals or venture capitalists) who provide capital financing to small businesses in exchange for equity shares or convertible debt. Angel investors can provide small business owners with the capital needed to launch their business, if they are willing to give a stake in their company in exchange for the funding. It is important that any business entering into an agreement with an angel investor thoroughly understands the terms and conditions of their agreement, as well as the risks associated with the agreement.

Venture capital firms are another source of small business funding. Venture capital firms specialize in lending money to new and emerging businesses in exchange for equity or convertible debt. Venture capital firms are often looking for businesses with a strong potential for growth and profitability. As such, venture capital firms typically take on more risk than other lenders, but they can also provide significant amounts of capital to start or grow a business.

Government grants are a final source of small business funding, and the most desirable option as businesses do not need to repay the money they receive in grants. Unfortunately, these grants are often highly competitive and difficult to qualify for, so getting a grant can be challenging. Business owners who pursue government grants should be prepared to submit a thorough business plan and to show the government that their business is viable and has the potential to succeed.

In addition to these traditional sources of funding, business owners may also be able to secure funding from other sources as well. These could include crowdfunding campaigns, family and friends, or even personal loans. It is important for business owners to shop around and explore all of their options in order to find the best deal for them and their business.

Securing funding for a small business can be a difficult and lengthy process. Business owners need to weigh all of their options to find the best solution for their situation, as each source of funding has its own benefits and drawbacks. With hard work and dedication, however, any business owner can find the right funding to get their business off the ground and running successfully.

Self-Financing Options

Starting a small business often requires financial resources to cover various expenses such as equipment, inventory, marketing, and operating costs. While there are external funding options available, such as loans and investors, many entrepreneurs prefer to self-finance their startups to maintain control and avoid debt or equity obligations. Self-financing allows business owners to utilize their own personal resources or generate funds internally. In this article, we will explore some common self-financing options for small business startups.

Personal Savings: One of the most straightforward self-financing options is to use personal savings. If you have accumulated savings over time, you can allocate a portion of it to fund your startup. While this method allows you to retain complete ownership and control over your business, it's important to consider the risks associated with depleting your personal funds and the potential impact on your personal financial stability.

Home Equity Loans or Lines of Credit: If you own a home, you may have the option to tap into its equity to finance your business. Home equity loans or lines of credit allow you to borrow against the value of your property. These loans often offer lower interest rates compared to other forms of borrowing, making them an attractive option. However, keep in mind that your home is used as collateral, so failure to repay the loan could result in the loss of your property.

Personal Credit Cards: While it's generally not recommended to rely solely on credit cards for financing a business, they can be a short-term solution for covering immediate expenses. Credit cards provide quick access to funds and often offer introductory periods with low or no interest rates. However, it's crucial to manage your credit card usage carefully and pay off balances promptly to avoid high-interest charges and accumulating debt.

Friends and Family: Turning to friends and family for financial support is a common option for small business startups. This approach allows you to borrow money or receive investments from people who trust and believe in your business idea. When pursuing this avenue, it's crucial to approach it professionally by creating clear agreements and treating the investment as a formal business transaction. Clearly define the terms, repayment plans, and potential risks involved to maintain healthy relationships with your loved ones.

Retirement Funds: Another self-financing option is to tap into retirement funds, such as a 401(k) or individual retirement account (IRA). Some retirement plans allow for penalty-free withdrawals or loans for business purposes. While this method provides access to capital, it's essential to consider the long-term consequences of depleting your retirement savings. Consult with a financial advisor to understand the potential tax implications and explore alternative strategies to minimize risks.

Crowdfunding: In recent years, crowdfunding has gained significant popularity as a means of raising funds for startups. Crowdfunding platforms allow entrepreneurs to showcase their business ideas and attract a broad base of individual investors who contribute small amounts of money. In return, contributors may receive rewards or early access to products and services. Crowdfunding not only provides capital but also helps validate your business concept and build a community of supporters.

Bootstrapping: Bootstrapping involves starting and growing a business with minimal external resources. This method requires entrepreneurs to be resourceful, frugal, and creative in managing their finances. Bootstrapping strategies may include using free or low-cost tools, leveraging personal networks for marketing, or bartering services with other businesses. While bootstrapping can be challenging, it allows you to maintain full control and equity in your business.

Vendor Financing: Some suppliers or vendors may offer financing options to their customers. This arrangement typically involves extending credit terms, allowing you to defer payment for goods or services until after you have generated revenue. Vendor financing can help conserve your initial cash flow and provide flexibility in managing your startup expenses

Seeking External Financing

One of the most critical aspects of launching a successful startup is securing adequate financing. While there are various options available, seeking external financing is a common route for many entrepreneurs. External financing refers to obtaining funds from outside sources, such as investors, banks, or government programs. We'll explore the process of seeking external financing for a small business startup and provides valuable insights for entrepreneurs.

Understand Your Funding Needs: Before embarking on the journey of seeking external financing, it is crucial to determine the specific funding requirements of your small business startup. Assess your financial needs based on factors such as business plan, operational costs, equipment, marketing, and working capital. Having a clear understanding of the amount of funding required will help you narrow down the appropriate financing options and approach potential investors or lenders with a well-defined proposal.

Develop a Solid Business Plan: A comprehensive and well-structured business plan is essential when seeking external financing. It acts as a roadmap for your business and demonstrates to investors or lenders that you have a clear vision, understand your target market, and have a strategy for success. Your business plan should include an executive summary, company description, market analysis, product/service description, marketing and sales strategies, financial projections, and an overview of the management team. A compelling business plan increases your chances of securing external financing.

Explore Different External Financing Options: There are several external financing options available for small business startups. These include:

a. Equity Financing: Equity financing involves selling ownership shares in your company to investors in exchange for capital. Venture capital firms, angel investors, and crowdfunding platforms are common sources of equity financing. These investors typically provide not only funds but also guidance and industry connections. However, giving up a portion of your ownership and control is a trade-off when opting for equity financing.

b. Debt Financing: Debt financing involves borrowing funds from lenders, such as banks or online lending platforms, with the obligation to repay the borrowed amount plus interest over a specific period. Traditional business loans, lines of credit, and Small Business Administration (SBA) loans are examples of debt financing. While debt financing allows you to retain full ownership and control of your business, it requires timely repayment and the ability to manage debt obligations.

c. Grants and Subsidies: Government agencies, non-profit organizations, and foundations offer grants and subsidies to support small businesses. These funding options often have specific eligibility criteria and focus on particular industries or causes. Research and identify grant opportunities that align with your business and explore the application process. Grants and subsidies can provide valuable non-dilutive capital for your startup.

d. Bootstrapping: Bootstrapping involves self-funding your startup using personal savings, credit cards, or revenue generated from the business. While this approach may limit your initial growth potential, it allows you to retain complete ownership and decision-making control. Bootstrapping can be a viable option for small-scale startups or those in industries with lower capital requirements.

Prepare a Compelling Pitch: When approaching potential investors or lenders, it is essential to prepare a compelling pitch that showcases the value proposition and potential of your small business startup. Craft a concise and persuasive pitch deck that highlights key aspects of your business, such as market opportunity, unique selling points, competitive advantage, financial projections, and the potential return on investment. Tailor your pitch to the specific interests and requirements of each investor or lender to demonstrate that you have done your homework and are serious about securing external financing.

Build Relationships and Network: Networking plays a crucial role in the process of seeking external financing. Attend industry events, join entrepreneur networks, and participate in pitch competitions to connect with potential investors and lenders. Building relationships and establishing trust is essential, as external

Exploring Government Programs and Grants

While traditional sources of financing such as loans and personal savings are commonly used, government programs and grants can offer an attractive alternative. This article aims to explore the various government programs and grant sources available to small business startups, highlighting their benefits, eligibility criteria, and application processes.

Small Business Administration (SBA) Programs: The Small Business Administration (SBA) is a key resource for entrepreneurs seeking funding and support. It offers several programs tailored to the needs of small business startups, including:

a. 7(a) Loan Program: The flagship program of the SBA, it provides loans for various purposes, including working capital, equipment purchases, and real estate acquisition. The loans are administered through SBA-approved lenders, with favorable terms and lower down payments.

b. Microloan Program: This program provides small loans, typically up to $50,000, to help entrepreneurs establish or expand their businesses. Microloans are administered through nonprofit organizations and community-based lenders, with additional technical assistance and support.

c. Small Business Investment Company (SBIC) Program: SBICs are privately owned and managed investment firms licensed and regulated by the SBA. They provide equity financing and long-term loans to small businesses. SBICs can be a valuable funding source, particularly for high-growth startups.

Federal Grant Programs: The U.S. federal government offers various grant programs to stimulate economic growth and support small businesses. Some notable grant sources include:

a. Small Business Innovation Research (SBIR) and Small Business Technology Transfer (STTR) Programs: These programs provide grants to small businesses engaged in research and development (R&D) with the potential for commercialization. The grants are awarded by federal agencies in specific areas, such as healthcare, energy, and defense.

b. Community Development Block Grants (CDBG): CDBG grants are provided to state and local governments, who then allocate funds to support economic development projects, including small business startups. These grants aim to create jobs and improve communities through infrastructure development and business assistance programs.

c. Economic Development Administration (EDA) Grants: The EDA offers grants to promote regional economic development. Their funding programs focus on job creation, infrastructure improvements, and fostering innovation and entrepreneurship. Small businesses can benefit from EDA grants through partnerships with local economic development organizations.

State and Local Government Programs: Beyond federal programs, state and local governments also provide a range of programs to support small business startups. These programs vary by location but commonly include:

a. Small Business Development Centers (SBDCs): SBDCs are funded by state and local governments in partnership with universities and the SBA. They offer free or low-cost business consulting services, training, and access to resources, helping startups navigate funding options and develop their business plans.

b. Business Incubators and Accelerators: Many states and municipalities operate business incubators and accelerators that provide physical space, mentorship, and networking opportunities to early-stage startups. Some incubators also offer funding, either through direct grants or connections to investors.

c. Tax Incentive Programs: To attract and support small businesses, states and localities often offer tax incentives, such as tax credits, exemptions, or reduced rates. These incentives can significantly reduce the financial burden for startups and encourage growth.

Chapter Five

Financial Recordkeeping and Bookkeeping

Starting a small business can be an exciting endeavor, but it also comes with a range of responsibilities, including financial record keeping and bookkeeping. Properly managing your company's finances is crucial for its success and growth. This guide aims to provide small business startups with a comprehensive understanding of financial record keeping and bookkeeping, emphasizing their importance and offering practical tips for effective implementation.

Importance of Financial Record Keeping:

Compliance: Maintaining accurate financial records is essential to comply with legal and regulatory requirements. It helps ensure that your business meets tax obligations and avoids penalties or audits.

Decision-making: Reliable financial records enable informed decision-making by providing insights into your business's financial health. It allows you to analyze profitability, identify trends, and make strategic adjustments to optimize operations.

Investor Relations: If you seek funding or partnerships, potential investors and partners will evaluate your financial records. Clear and organized financial documentation enhances credibility and increases the chances of securing investment or forming valuable partnerships.

Tracking Business Performance: By tracking income, expenses, and other financial metrics, you can monitor your business's performance over time. This information facilitates the identification of strengths, weaknesses, and areas requiring improvement.

Key Components of Financial Record Keeping:

Income Records: Keep track of all revenue sources, including sales, services, and investments. Utilize a system that captures detailed information, such as customer names, transaction dates, and payment methods.

Expense Records: Record all business-related expenses, such as rent, utilities, supplies, and employee salaries. Maintain supporting documents, such as receipts and invoices, to substantiate your expenses.

Cash Flow Management: Regularly monitor cash flow by tracking incoming and outgoing funds. This allows you to anticipate periods of low cash flow and take necessary measures to avoid financial strain.

Accounts Receivable and Payable: Keep records of money owed to your business (accounts receivable) and money owed by your business (accounts payable). Timely management of these accounts helps maintain positive relationships with suppliers and customers.

Tax Records: Maintain accurate and organized tax records, including income statements, receipts, and expense records. Consult with a tax professional to ensure compliance with tax laws and regulations specific to your jurisdiction.

Implementing Effective Bookkeeping Practices:

Separate Business and Personal Finances: Open a dedicated business bank account and use it exclusively for business transactions. This separation simplifies bookkeeping, reduces confusion, and helps you track business-related income and expenses more accurately.

Choose a Bookkeeping System: Select a bookkeeping system that aligns with your business needs. Options include manual record keeping, spreadsheets, or accounting software. Consider factors such as cost, complexity, scalability, and reporting capabilities.

Organize and Classify Transactions: Establish a logical system for organizing and categorizing financial transactions. Create separate accounts for different types of income and expenses, ensuring consistency and ease of reporting.

Maintain Accurate Financial Statements: Prepare regular financial statements, including income statements, balance sheets, and cash flow statements. These statements provide an overview of your business's financial position and performance, helping you make informed decisions.

Reconcile Bank Statements: Regularly reconcile your business bank statements with your financial records. This process ensures that all transactions are accurately recorded and helps identify discrepancies or errors.

Track Inventory: If your business involves selling physical products, implement an inventory management system. Keep records of inventory levels, costs, and sales to effectively manage stock and prevent stockouts or overstocking.

Regularly Review Financial Records: Set aside time to review your financial records regularly. This practice allows you to spot potential issues, address errors promptly, and make informed decisions based on accurate financial information.

Setting Up an Effective Bookkeeping System

Implementing an effective bookkeeping system from the beginning is crucial for the success and growth of your startup. In this guide, we will outline the key steps to setting up a bookkeeping system that will help you stay organized, make informed financial decisions, and ensure compliance with tax regulations.

Steps of setting up bookkeeping

1. Choose an Accounting Method: The first step in setting up your bookkeeping system is to choose an accounting method. There are two popular

methods: cash basis and accrual basis. The cash basis method records income and expenses when cash is received or paid, respectively. Regardless of when money actually exchanges hands, the accrual basis technique records income and expenses as they are incurred. Consider the nature of your business and consult with a professional accountant to determine the most suitable method for your startup.

2. Set Up a Chart of Accounts: A chart of accounts is a categorized list of all the accounts used in your bookkeeping system. It provides a structure for organizing your financial transactions. Start by identifying the main categories relevant to your business, such as revenue, expenses, assets, liabilities, and equity. Within each category, create specific accounts that reflect the different aspects of your business. Common accounts include sales, inventory, rent, utilities, salaries, and loans. Using accounting software can simplify the process of setting up and managing your chart of accounts.

3. Choose Bookkeeping Software: Investing in reliable bookkeeping software can streamline your financial management processes. Look for software that offers essential features such as invoicing, expense tracking, bank reconciliation, financial reporting, and tax preparation. Popular

options include QuickBooks, Xero, and FreshBooks. Consider your budget, scalability needs, and integration capabilities with other software tools you may be using.

4. Establish a Systematic Record-Keeping Process: Consistency is key when it comes to bookkeeping. Develop a systematic record-keeping process that ensures all financial transactions are accurately recorded and organized. Create a filing system for physical documents, such as invoices, receipts, and bank statements, and implement a digital filing system for electronic documents. Clearly label and store these records in a secure and easily accessible location.

5. Separate Personal and Business Finances: To maintain accurate financial records and simplify tax reporting, it is crucial to separate your personal and business finances. Open a dedicated business bank account to handle all business-related income and expenses. Use this account exclusively for your business transactions and avoid mixing personal funds with business funds. Additionally, consider obtaining a business credit card to further separate personal and business expenses.

6. Track Income and Expenses: Consistently tracking your income and expenses is essential

for understanding the financial health of your startup. Record all sources of income, including sales revenue, loans, and investments. Categorize your expenses based on your chart of accounts and regularly update your records. Track both fixed expenses (e.g., rent, utilities) and variable expenses (e.g., inventory, marketing). To verify accuracy, compare your records to your bank statements.

7. Perform Regular Bank Reconciliations: Bank reconciliations are critical for identifying any discrepancies between your records and your bank statements. Regularly reconcile your bank accounts by comparing your recorded transactions with those provided by your bank. This process helps detect errors, such as missing or duplicate transactions, and ensures that your financial records align with your actual bank balances.

8. Implement Invoicing and Accounts Receivable Processes: Efficiently managing your receivables is crucial for maintaining a healthy cash flow. Develop an invoicing process that includes clear payment terms, due dates, and accepted payment methods. Send invoices right once and pursue any unpaid balances

Tracking Income and Expenses

Starting a small business can be an exciting endeavor, but it also comes with a multitude of responsibilities, including effectively tracking income and expenses. Managing your finances is crucial for the success and sustainability of your business. Accurate and organized financial records provide valuable insights into your business's financial health, help with tax compliance, and enable informed decision-making. In this article, we will explore the importance of tracking income and expenses for a small business startup and provide practical tips to do it effectively.

Why is tracking income and expenses important?

Financial Awareness: Tracking income and expenses allows you to gain a comprehensive understanding of your business's financial health. It helps you determine whether your business is generating enough revenue to cover expenses and make a profit. By analyzing your financial records, you can identify areas where you can cut costs, increase revenue, or improve efficiency.

Tax Compliance: Accurate income and expense tracking are essential for fulfilling your tax obligations. Proper record-keeping ensures that you report your income correctly and claim all eligible deductions. This practice will help you avoid penalties, audits, and potential legal issues with tax authorities. Moreover, well-maintained financial records make the tax preparation process smoother and less time-consuming.

Decision Making: Tracking income and expenses provides the necessary data to make informed business decisions. When you have a clear picture of your financial situation, you can evaluate the feasibility of new investments, assess the profitability of different products or services, and identify areas where cost-cutting measures can be implemented. This financial insight enables you to make strategic decisions that can lead to long-term business growth and success.

Tips for effective income and expense tracking:
Separate Business and Personal Finances: Establish a clear separation between your personal and business finances. Create a separate business bank account and only conduct business transactions through it. This separation makes it easier to track and analyze your business's financial activities, simplifies tax preparation, and enhances the credibility of your business.

Choose a Bookkeeping System: Select a bookkeeping system that suits the needs of your business. There are various options available, including manual spreadsheets, desktop accounting software, and cloud-based solutions. Consider factors such as cost, ease of use, scalability, and integration with other business tools.

For small businesses, popular options for accounting software include QuickBooks, Xero, and FreshBooks.

Maintain Detailed Records: Keep detailed records of all your income and expenses. Create a filing system to organize receipts, invoices, bank statements, and any other financial documents. Regularly update your records to ensure accuracy and completeness. The more organized your financial records are, the easier it will be to track and analyze your business's financial performance.

Track Income Sources: Monitor and categorize all sources of income. Whether it's revenue from product sales, services rendered, or investments, record each transaction accurately and assign it to the appropriate income category. This level of tracking enables you to identify your most profitable revenue streams and focus your efforts on maximizing their potential.

Categorize Expenses: Categorize your expenses to gain visibility into your spending patterns. Common expense categories include rent, utilities, inventory, marketing, salaries, and professional services. Assign each expense to the relevant category to understand where your money is going and identify areas where you can optimize your spending.

Reconcile Bank Statements: Regularly reconcile your business bank statements with your financial records. This process involves comparing your recorded transactions with the transactions listed on your bank statement to ensure accuracy and identify any discrepancies. Reconciliation helps you catch errors, detect fraudulent activities, and maintain the integrity of your financial data.

Monitor Cash Flow: Track your cash flow closely to understand the timing and movement of money in your business. Cash flow management is crucial for ensuring you have enough funds to cover expenses, pay employees, and invest in growth opportunities. Analyze your cash flow statements regularly to identify any potential cash flow gaps and take proactive measures to address them.

Implement a Budget: Create a budget for your business to plan and control your expenses. A budget sets spending limits, helps you prioritize investments, and ensures you allocate resources effectively. Monitor your actual expenses against the budgeted amounts and make adjustments as necessary. This practice helps you stay on track and avoid overspending.

Leverage Technology: Take advantage of technology to streamline your income and expense tracking processes. Many accounting software solutions offer features like automatic bank feeds, receipt scanning, and financial reporting. These tools can save you time, reduce errors, and provide real-time insights into your financial performance.

Seek Professional Help if Needed: If managing your finances becomes overwhelming or you lack expertise in accounting, consider hiring a professional bookkeeper or accountant. They can help set up your financial systems, ensure compliance with tax regulations, and provide valuable advice on financial matters. Outsourcing this function allows you to focus on running your business while ensuring your finances are in capable hands.

Tracking income and expenses is a vital practice for small business startups. It enables you to maintain financial awareness, comply with tax regulations, and make informed decisions. By implementing effective tracking methods and leveraging technology, you can maintain accurate financial records, monitor your business's financial health, and pave the way for long-term success. Remember, organized finances contribute to the stability and growth of your business, so make it a priority from the early stages and reap the benefits in the future.

Maintaining Accurate Financial Records

Accurate financial records are crucial for the success of any small business startup. Whether you are a sole proprietorship, a partnership, or a limited liability company, keeping track of your financial transactions is essential for making informed decisions, complying with tax obligations, securing financing, and demonstrating the financial health of your business. In this article, we will explore the importance of maintaining accurate financial records and provide practical tips on how to do so effectively.

Importance of Accurate Financial Records

Accurate financial records serve as the foundation for managing your business's finances effectively. Here are some key reasons why maintaining accurate financial records is vital for small business startups:

a. Decision-Making: Accurate financial records provide you with the necessary information to make informed decisions about your business operations. They help you understand your revenue streams, expenses, and profitability, enabling you to identify areas of improvement and develop strategies for growth.

b. Tax Compliance: Maintaining accurate financial records is crucial for fulfilling your tax obligations. Complete and organized records allow you to accurately report your income and expenses, claim deductions, and meet filing deadlines, reducing the risk of penalties and audits.

c. Financial Planning: Accurate financial records enable you to develop realistic budgets, set financial goals, and plan for future growth. They help you identify trends, forecast cash flow, and assess the financial viability of new projects or investments.

d. Investor and Lender Confidence: If you seek external funding, such as loans or investments, accurate financial records are essential. Potential investors and lenders will review your financial statements to evaluate the financial health and performance of your business. Accurate records demonstrate your credibility and instill confidence in stakeholders.

e. Business Valuation: Accurate financial records are crucial when valuing your business for potential sale, merger, or acquisition. A detailed record of your financial transactions provides a clear picture of your business's value, making the negotiation process smoother and more accurate.

Key Financial Records to Maintain

To maintain accurate financial records, there are several key documents and records you should track. Here are some essential financial records for small business startups:

a. Income and Sales Records: Keep a record of all sales transactions, including invoices, sales receipts, and cash register tapes. These documents should detail the date, customer name, item or service sold, quantity, price, and payment method.

b. Expense Receipts: Keep receipts for all business-related expenses, such as office supplies, rent, utilities, marketing expenses, and travel costs. Categorize and organize these receipts to facilitate accurate expense tracking.

c. Bank Statements: Regularly reconcile your bank statements with your internal records to ensure accuracy. Reconciling involves comparing your bank transactions to your own records to identify any discrepancies or errors.

d. Payroll Records: If you have employees, maintain accurate payroll records, including timesheets, wage rates, tax withholdings, benefits, and any other relevant information. Compliance with payroll regulations is essential to avoid legal and financial penalties.

e. Tax Records: Keep copies of filed tax returns, supporting documentation, and relevant tax forms. This includes income tax returns, sales tax returns, payroll tax returns, and any other applicable tax filings.

f. Financial Statements: Prepare regular financial statements, such as income statements (profit and loss statements), balance sheets, and cash flow statements. These statements provide an overview of your business's financial performance and position.

Tips for Maintaining Accurate Financial Records

Maintaining accurate financial records may seem overwhelming, but with proper systems and practices in place, it can be streamlined. Here are some practical tips to help you maintain accurate financial records for your small business startup:

a. Use Accounting Software: Consider using accounting software to streamline your record-keeping process. Software solutions like QuickBooks, Xero, or FreshBooks automate various accounting tasks, making it easier to track income, expenses, and generate financial statements.

b. Implement a Chart of Accounts: Develop a chart of accounts tailored to your business. A chart of accounts is a categorized list of all the accounts you use to track your financial transactions. It provides structure and consistency to your record-keeping process.

c. Regularly Reconcile Bank Accounts: Set a schedule to reconcile your bank accounts on a monthly basis. Compare your internal records to your bank statements, ensuring that all transactions are accounted for and any discrepancies are resolved promptly.

d. Separate Business and Personal Finances: Maintain separate bank accounts and credit cards for your business and personal finances. Mixing personal and business transactions can lead to confusion and complicate accurate record-keeping.

e. Organize and Store Documents: Establish a filing system for your financial documents. Store physical copies or scan and save electronic copies of receipts, invoices, bank statements, and other relevant records in an organized manner. This will facilitate easy retrieval and audit preparation.

f. Backup Your Data: Regularly back up your financial data to prevent the loss of critical information. Cloud-based storage solutions or external hard drives can be used to secure your data and protect it from potential hardware failures or disasters.

g. Seek Professional Help if Needed: If you find it challenging to manage your financial records or lack the necessary expertise, consider seeking professional help. Hiring an accountant or bookkeeper can ensure accuracy and provide valuable insights into your financial management.

Maintaining accurate financial records is essential for the success and growth of small business startups. Accurate records support decision-making, tax compliance, financial planning, investor confidence, and business valuation. By establishing effective systems, using accounting software, and adhering to best practices, you can ensure your financial records are accurate, organized, and readily available when needed. Remember, accurate financial records are not only a legal obligation but also a powerful tool to drive the financial success of your small business startup.

Conclusion

Financial planning is a critical aspect of starting a small business. It involves developing a comprehensive strategy to manage the company's finances effectively and ensure long-term success. Throughout this essay, we have explored various key elements of financial planning for small business startups. Now, in conclusion, let us summarize the main points and emphasize the significance of financial planning in this context.

First and foremost, financial planning provides a roadmap for small business owners, guiding them towards their financial goals. By setting clear objectives and outlining the steps needed to achieve them, entrepreneurs can stay focused and make informed decisions. It helps in prioritizing actions and allocating resources appropriately, ensuring that limited funds are directed to areas that generate the highest return on investment.

One of the fundamental aspects of financial planning is budgeting. Creating a detailed budget allows entrepreneurs to track and control their expenditures, identify areas of overspending, and make necessary adjustments. A well-crafted budget helps in avoiding financial pitfalls and maintaining financial discipline. It serves as a benchmark to measure the company's performance against projections and enables timely corrective actions if deviations occur.

Cash flow management is another critical component of financial planning for small business startups. Effective cash flow management ensures that there is enough liquidity to cover operational expenses and meet financial obligations. It involves monitoring cash inflows and outflows, predicting cash needs, and implementing strategies to optimize cash flow. This proactive approach prevents cash shortages and enables businesses to seize growth opportunities or navigate through challenging times.

Furthermore, financial planning assists small business owners in making informed investment decisions. Whether it's purchasing equipment, expanding operations, or exploring new markets, having a solid financial plan helps in evaluating the feasibility and potential returns of investment opportunities. By conducting thorough financial analysis, entrepreneurs can assess the financial viability and risks associated with each investment, thereby minimizing the chances of making costly mistakes.

In addition to internal decision-making, financial planning is essential for external stakeholders such as lenders and investors. When seeking funding or partnerships, small business owners must present a comprehensive financial plan that demonstrates their understanding of the company's financial health and future prospects. A well-prepared plan increases the likelihood of securing financing and instills confidence in potential investors or partners, fostering mutually beneficial relationships.

Risk management is yet another critical aspect of financial planning. Starting a small business involves inherent risks, and a comprehensive financial plan incorporates strategies to mitigate those risks. It involves identifying potential threats, such as economic downturns or industry-specific challenges, and developing contingency plans to minimize their impact. By considering different risk scenarios and implementing appropriate risk management strategies, entrepreneurs can safeguard their businesses and improve resilience.

Moreover, financial planning encourages entrepreneurs to prioritize saving and investing for the future. By setting aside a portion of profits for reinvestment or building a contingency fund, small businesses can create a cushion to withstand unexpected expenses or capitalize on growth opportunities. Financial planning helps strike a balance between short-term needs and long-term objectives, ensuring sustainable growth and long-term success.

Finally, financial planning enables small business owners to evaluate their progress and make necessary adjustments along the way. By regularly reviewing financial statements, key performance indicators, and other relevant metrics, entrepreneurs can assess the effectiveness of their strategies and identify areas for improvement. This iterative process of monitoring and adapting helps small businesses stay agile and responsive in a dynamic market environment.

Financial planning is crucial for the success of small business startups. It offers a road map for business owners, assisting them in setting objectives, selecting wisely, and allocating resources. Budgeting, cash flow management, investment analysis, risk management, and savings planning are all integral components of financial planning. By incorporating these elements into their overall business strategy, entrepreneurs can enhance their chances of success, secure funding, and navigate challenges with confidence. Therefore, every small business startup should prioritize financial planning as a fundamental pillar of their operations.

www.ingramcontent.com/pod-product-compliance
Lightning Source LLC
Chambersburg PA
CBHW070452220526
45466CB00004B/1806